EYES HAVE NOT SEEN!.....

EARS HAVE NOT HEARD!.....

Michelle Whitmore

Unless otherwise noted, Scripture quotations are from the King James Version of the Bible. Copyright © 1979, 1980, 1982 by Thomas Nelson, Inc., Publishers.

References from Webster's New World Dictionary, Pocket Books Paperback Edition. Copyright © 2003. By Wiley Publishing Inc.

References from: https://en.wikipedia.org/wiki/Posttraumatic_stress_disorder

ISBN-10: 069264119X
ISBN-13: 978-0692641194

DEDICATION

This book is dedicated to my daughter, Chayil. I love you so much and will forever love you! You are a gift from God, a woman of virtue. You are so special to me. I pray that this book continues to bless me and help me to continue to be a whole mother in order to raise a whole daughter. I also pray that this book will bless you in your future. My hope is that it will help you to dream and see the manifestation of your dreams. You will reach your blessed purpose in life that God has ordained for you! I pray that I leave an honorable legacy behind to help others and bless you far beyond my time here on earth. Love always, Mommy.

Contents

Acknowledgements

To God: Thank you God for your favor on me. Thank you God for covering me with your blood, grace and mercy. Thank you for covering my family. Thank you for your gift of Chayil to me. You are my savior, my friend, my father, my provider, my source, my peace, my joy, my strength, my everything. I love you!

To the People of God: This book is for those who want to see the manifestation of the power of God in your lives according to your faith. This book is to give you guidance on how to purge yourself from insecurities and curses that have plagued your life. It is to show you biblically how to fill your vessel up with strength and confidence according to what God your creator has said about you in his **word** (the bible). I pray that you find deliverance for your life, and pursue your purpose with assurance that God is with you, he will keep you and cause you to prosper. I further pray that you reach back and help someone else get delivered from the shackles, lies, distress, curses, oppression, and captivity that they have been living with in their hearts and minds. God is Love. God is Peace. God IS!....... whatever we need him to be. Let's take full advantage of this moment to explore how to live in the full permissions of liberty that God intended for us. I love you!

Bless God for his grace and mercy endures forever!

i

Introduction

Many people have unbelievable, heart wrenching life stories that leave others speechless. I too have a story. It is not to leave you speechless but to dare you to begin thinking about the important critical, life changing, life altering, decisions you make and explore how you come up with those decisions. Ten years ago I started to write this book to first tell my story and second to help others who deal with or have dealt with some of the same issues that I have experienced such as: **abandonment, uselessness, low self-esteem, rejection** and so much more that causes us to make poor decisions. This is an incredible journey that both you and I are about to go on together.

I did not write this book to compete with other's stories or put people to shame. I authored this book because so many people have been told "lies" their entire life which they consciously or subconsciously believe. Whether one subconsciously or consciously believes these untruths, eventually they manifest themselves into decisions that we make which drastically affect and influence our lives. What is a lie? "A false statement made with intent to deceive." (Webster's New World Dictionary pg. 373) Only the spirit of satan will lie to you with the intent of deception. God will never lie to you. "God is not a man that he should lie; neither the son of man, that he should repent." (Numbers 23:19) Together, we are going to navigate how to change the course of our lives by relying on the **word** of God to dictate our success.

Theme Scripture: The **word** of **God** says, "In the beginning was the **Word** and the **Word** was with **God**, and the **Word** was **God**." (John 1:1)

Part I

YOU SAY...

Chapter One

Lots of Love? or Lies of Life?

There were times in life where in my mind, I did not know if I was going or coming. My mind was causing me to trigger emotions and make poor decisions that I immediately regretted. What I have come to realize is that you do not get to this place called "here/present/reality" by yourself but you get to this place from your upbringing, interaction with family, friends, and through life experiences. Have you ever heard about the emoji "LOL"? I have come to realize that the simple abbreviation "LOL" does not always mean well. LOL – is often known as 1) Laughing out Loud or 2) Lots of love. It has been used for years often at the end of text messages and e-mails. It is the most used expression by people who communicate via e-mail and text. For this purpose we will focus on "Lots of Love".

Often times people throw out the emoji "LOL" in an attempt to signify Lots of Love. Is this what they really mean? Are they saying that they love you? And if so, to what extent do they love you? And if they love you, how much trust do you put in them simply because they said "LOL" giving the expression that they love you? Do you hang on their every **word** because you believe that they love you? Do you measure your value based on their opinion of you or what they say about you simply because they say they love you "LOL".

I say that "LOL" can be translated into "Lies of Life". At some point in life have you ever asked yourself the question, how did I become like this? What is my purpose? Will I ever live out my true purpose? Am I a productive individual? Am I living within my true self? Do I have joy? Do I have peace? What have I accomplished in life? Have I helped people and society in general? What legacy will I leave behind?

Do we want our lives to simply be abbreviated "LOL"? I came to a point in life where I realized that I needed help and could no longer live with so many uncertainties. I felt like I was just going through the motions, running the rat race and going in circles. I repeated the same mistakes over and over. I was always asking "why me"? I made excuses to explain away why I wasn't yet living out my true purpose. I blamed past interactions with acquaintances, friends, family, past relationships and previous life experiences for my delay. Now while it is very true that these experiences created major barriers in my development, put me on wrong paths, caused me to be bitter, tainted, and misguided, at the end of the day the responsibility rest with me to overcome those barriers. I became accountable to break the spirit of bondage off of my life in order to be free and live out my true purpose. It was up to me to find my rightful power through recognizing who my creator (God) designed me to be and the power that he placed inside of me through his **word**. I once heard a saying, but I'm not sure where it originated….."If you want to know the purposed of a thing, ask the creator." (Author –unknown)

Now let's delve and deal with some of my "Lies of Life" which I am sure that some of you share so that we can begin to live in truth. 'And ye shall know the truth, and the truth shall make you free" (John 8:32)

Let's look at 3 different stages of life where lies have had the propensity to trail blaze us down the wrong path.

1. ***Childhood*** – Lies told to you as a child that assisted in shaping your future.

E.g.: When a child does something wrong that reminds a grown-up of negative aspects seen in their father or mother, sometimes the child is told: "You are just like your father!" or "You are just like your mother!"

<u>Points to Ponder.......</u>

a. There is no way that a child can be just like a grown man or woman. However, the individual who consistently tells the child this "lie" has now stamped and sealed in the child's mind that they are just like their father and/or mother. The child will now either subconsciously or consciously begin to take on the traits of the parental figure. There is an important question to ask ourselves.....Can a 4 year old or 9 year old child be a whore, drunk, voluntary drug user, alcoholic, and pedophile? NO.

b. What if the parent is a horrible person? Does that make the child a horrible person as well?

c. What if the child grows up taking on tendencies like the father or mother? Now the child becomes labeled by everyone as being just like their father or mother instead of having their own identity.

d. What if the child pattern's their parent's behavior which is often what children do because they learn by example? Children do not know how to distinguish between behaviors that they should model and behaviors they should not model. They repeat what they observe. Does this predetermine that they are going to be an exact replica of their parent? Or does this just mean that they are temporarily misguided?

Do you see how a poor choice of **word**s can unknowingly mislead a person to carry on a generational curse within their family? The devil is very happy when you help him to carry on these demonic curses because you have just made his job easier which is to steal, kill, and destroy. "The thief cometh not, but for to steal, and to kill, and to destroy: I am come that they might have life, and that they might have it more abundantly." (John 10:10) The devil will try to destroy your life by making you feel like only negative things happen to you again and again. He comes to kill your dreams starting from youth by making you feel that you are limited to walk in someone else's shoes and not fulfill your own vision and destiny. He also comes to rob your faith surrounding your goals and desires. "Be sober, be vigilant; because your adversary the devil, as a roaring lion, walketh about, seeking whom he may devour." (I Peter 5:8)

You must remember, that in the **word** of God it says, "I am come that they might have life, and that they might have it more abundantly." (John 10:10) You have all the power that God put within you to be who God called you to be and live an abundant life.

2. *Young Adult* – Lies told to you as a young adult that assisted in shaping your present state and future.

E.g.: I remember as a young adult, I used to date this guy and when I cooked for him he would say that I couldn't cook. The more he said it the less I cooked. The less motivated I became, the less effort I put into cooking, therefore making heartless, tasteless, meals. After that relationship ended, I began dating someone new. Although leery at first, when I started cooking for him, he said "oh boy… you can cook! Your food is good!" Although I didn't have much faith in my skills at that time, his positive **word**s inspired me which led me to cook more and put more time and effort in. Now I can boldly say today that I am a great cook! "Death and life are in the power of the tongue." (Proverbs 18:21) Be careful about what you say. Speak positive things. Speak your dreams into existence. When your desires line up with God's will then you can ask what you may and it shall be so. "If ye shall ask any thing in my name, I will do it." (John 14:14). "Ye have not, because ye ask not" (James 4:2). Speak the **word** of God (bible). Your future rests inside of the **word** of God. "It is written, man shall not live by bread alone, but by every **word** that proceedeth out of the mouth of God." (Matthew 4:4)

The bible says. ."It is better to trust in the LORD than to put confidence in man." (Psalms 118:8) There is still time to change the direction of your life and see the manifestation of your dreams. Don't allow other people's **word**s to have power over you. You must take back your power, through the power that God gave you, and begin to "Calleth those things which be not as though they were." (Romans 4:17) As life proceeds, you must begin to believe in what the **word** of God says about you and the instructions it leaves for you. BIBLE some say means = Biblical Instructions Before leaving Earth. You must not always believe the **word**s which are sometimes untruths of people who say they love you. How do I know that you believe some of these lies, because your actions and decisions you make in life are based upon the lies that you have been told and not the truth which exists only in the **word** of God. You begin to believe that what they say about you is true. You unknowingly limit yourself to who they said you are and what they said you would become.

_3._   **_Adult_** – Lies told to you as an adult that assisted in shaping your present being.

At this point, as an adult people have told you things like…."Well it's too late to change. You can't teach an old dog new tricks. I'm too old to change. I'm set in my ways. This is how God made me. At times we as adults get set in our ways. Whether it is a poor attitude, handling our money irresponsibly, being a chronic gossiper, being a functioning drunk/alcoholic, shopaholic, hot tempered, keeping a dirty house, or having poor hygiene. These are all small examples of what some adults have inhabited for a lack of better **word**s called patterns, weaknesses, and addictions. People get settled in these bad habits and think that it's ok. Unfortunately many of us have more than one bad habit and when this happens you are definitely not living up to the full potential that God intended for you. Instead we have settled on what we think are inherited traits from our parents, aunts, friends, ect. We say to ourselves, well my mother always kept a bad house or was a chronic gossiper or had a bad temper and thus I inherited honestly. Well, this is yet another "Lie of Life" that we have accepted. These obstacles that you have chosen to accept are devouring your dreams and sucking your purpose right out of your future.

We are children of the most high God and must keep using God's **word** to fulfill our purpose in life. There is nothing honest or pure about bad behaviors. Listen, no one is perfect. I am not perfect. However, we must strive to be better. If God the father, the one who laid down his life so that his blood can make us whole exhibited many of these behaviors, would we still have faith in him and strive to be like him? Would we respect the awesome power and glory of God? How then do we expect others to respect us as children of God and acknowledge the favor and glory of God that rest on your life? We are blessed with grace that gives us another opportunity to improve. It is the grace of God that has allowed us to breathe yet another day in order to get better and do better.

Think about fulfilling your ultimate dream and purpose that will bring gratification to you both spiritually, mentally, and financially. In order to achieve that purpose can you please tell me where the multiple bad habits above would fit in nicely? Not too many places. There is no more room for excuses to not strive for excellence in what you do here on earth. Your name means more to the world and should carry greater significance and meaning than he/she is a drunk, gossiper, shopaholic, and hot tempered person. Throughout life these lies are what keep us bound, tired, depressed, stressed, anxious, and worried. Within this book we will navigate together on how to live in truth and freedom. "And you shall know the truth, and the truth shall make you free." (John 8:32) We are going to discuss, open up and explore some deeper issues within that many have difficulty with. We will deal with areas in life, which have troubled us in hopes to bring healing.

Don't allow satan to trick you into believing lies which will stifle your future, your destiny and your dreams. Let's look at an example of a lie that satan directed to mankind to cause us to be cursed in an attempt to destroy us.

Genesis 3: 2-13

2. And the woman said unto the serpent, We may eat of the fruit of the trees, of the garden:

3. But of the fruit of the tree which is in the midst of the garden, God hath said, Ye shall not eat of it, neither shall ye touch it, lest ye die.

4. And the serpent said unto the woman, Ye shall not surely die:

5. For God doth know that in the day ye eat thereof, then your eyes shall be opened, and ye shall be as gods, knowing good and evil.

6. And when the woman saw that the tree was good for food, and that it was pleasant to the eyes, and a tree to be desired to make one wise, she took of the fruit thereof, and did eat, and gave also unto her husband with her; and he did eat.

7. And the eyes of them both were opened, and they knew that they were naked; and they sewed fig leaves together, and made themselves aprons.

8. And they heard the voice of the Lord God walking in the garden in the cool of the day: and Adam and his wife hid themselves from the presence of the Lord God amongst the trees of the garden.

9. And the Lord God called unto Adam, and said unto him, Where art thou?

10. Ad he said, I heard thy voice in the garden, and I was afraid, because I was naked; and I hid myself.

11. And he said, Who told thee that thou wast naked? Hast thou eaten of the tree, whereof I command thee that thou shouldest not eat?

12. And the man said, The woman whom thou gavest to be with me, she gave me of the tree, and I did eat.

13. And the Lord God said unto the woman, What is this that thou hast done? And the woman said, The serpent beguilded me, and I did eat.

In verse 4 and 5 satan lies to Eve and said, that both she and her husband Adam will not die if they eat of the fruit tree that God told them not to eat from. He lied to them and said, the only reason God did not want them to eat of that tree was because their eyes would be open; they would be like Gods and know the difference between good and evil. Eve chose to believe that her eyes would be open in a positive way like Gods. She chose to believe that having this particular knowledge, that satan told her about was the way to go instead of listening to God. Eve then decided to eat the fruit and give some to her husband Adam. This did not cause them to physically perish, but mentally and spiritually die. They now became afraid and lived in fear instead of hope, favor and purpose which God intended for them. They now hid themselves and began to doubt themselves. Their hopes and dreams began to fade away and depart.

Prior to eating the fruit both Adam and Eve were covered by the glory of God. They were covered by the mercy and grace of God. It was after eating the fruit that they realized how vulnerable they were and God's mercy, glory and grace were no longer fully covering them at all times. They became fearful and felt naked, so they covered themselves not realizing that making a small apron from fig leaves would not protect them from the wiles of satan as God their creator did. God then asked them, who told you that you were naked? He also asked them if they had eaten of the tree that he instructed them not to eat of? Adam responded that Eve gave him of the fruit of the tree.

I want to tell you….. Don't eat the fruit! Don't believe the hype! Don't believe the lies! If you choose not to follow the **word**s of God which are found in the **word** of God/Bible, but choose to believe all of the lies that satan feeds you and your family, you can alter the path that your life takes in a negative way, become vulnerable, and loose the covering of

God's grace, mercy and glory. Don't eat of the fruit or the lies that satan tries to feed you or your family. He will tell you that you are not good enough and that you will never amount to be anything. He will tell you that you are worthless, stupid or a burden. As you can see if satan can get to those who are close to you as he did with Eve when Eve convinced Adam to eat, then he can get to you in that way as well. There will be others that you care about who satan will use to trick you. They do love you but they have been used of satan unknowingly to get to you. They have been used by him to try and convince you of lies, carry on generational curses, persuade you to take shortcuts in life, influence you to try and get you naked, vulnerable and cause your dreams to die. You have to do your best to say, those fig trees and that apron do not belong to me. I don't want that apron! That is not my garment to wear! There will never be an apron large enough to cover all of this body, all of this potential, purpose, destiny, ambition, and legacy that God has given me. Only God's glory, grace, mercy, blood, favor and love are enough to cover me.

"For the LORD God is a sun and shield: the LORD will give grace and glory: no good thing will he withhold from them that walk uprightly." (Psalms 84:11)

"But where sin abounded, grace did much more abound:" (Romans 5:20)

"In whom we have redemption through his blood, the forgiveness of sins, according to the riches of his grace;" (Ephesians 1:7)

"And his mercy is on them that fear him from generation to generation." (Luke 1:50)

"Surely goodness and mercy shall follow me all the days of my life: and I will dwell in the house of the LORD for ever." (Psalms 23:6)

Listen to what your creator God says to you and about you. He will never steer you wrong. He loves you and wants what is best for you!

Chapter Two:

Spirit of Abandonment

Background information: I was born a fatherless daughter of a mentally ill mother. I was told that I went into an orphanage somewhere between 4 days old and 6 months old. I stayed in an orphanage until 1 ½ at which point I became a foster child to a pastor and first lady. My biological family disclosed that my biological mother was diagnosed with a mental illness around the age of 15. She had a nervous breakdown in her early teenage years after her parents died within months of one another. I met my biological mother when I was 12 years old. Out of her own mouth she revealed to me that she felt rejected, abandoned and unloved by her surviving siblings. At around age 20 she wanted to feel loved so she decided to sleep with three Nigerian men in one weekend, who were on student visas. She told them that her intention was to get pregnant in order to have a child who would love her unconditionally and never reject her. All of the men complied, and so here I am. None of the men stuck around to find out if they were the father, who I was or what I would become. After I was born all three men went back to Nigeria with their wives and families never to be found again. My biological mother made a lot of poor decisions because of her illness. The confusion in her mind in conjunction with her emotions caused her to make these poor decisions. This is an example of "LOL" lies of life. Her mind told her lies that she was not loved and hence she made a poor decision to have a child in order to fill her empty space. I would later be taken from her as a baby, which caused a much greater void in her life. This is one example of how lies can cause us to create turmoil and turbulent situations that only God can get us out of and grant us complete healing from.

There are many stories about how I ended up being adopted. Let me tell you the one that I am the most familiar with. I was told that my biological mother was not able to adequately care for me due to her illness and unfortunately made decisions that caused her to loose me to the State of New Jersey. My biological family on my mother's side has very fair skin. Some can almost pass for Caucasian. My biological mother was also very light skinned. She had a complex with skin color. Due to my father being a dark skinned Nigerian man, my skin is a caramel brown color. According to my biological family, when I was born my birth mother tried to cut me open through my belly button because she said that she wanted her white baby back. I have a nice thin scar on my stomach stretching from my belly button to about 3 inches out. It has been there all of my life without explanation. My family also told me that my biological mother burned me in the face with an iron. They never gave an explanation as to why she did this but I have always had a burn mark on the left side of my face. According to my biological family I was taken away by the state at 6 months old and placed in an orphanage where I remained until I was about 1 ½. At five years old my foster parents chose to adopt me.

Annually, my adopted mother would send the adoption agency pictures of me to give to my biological mother. One year my adopted mom accidentally left my new first and last name on the back of the picture. It was at that point, my biological mother told the adoption agency that if they did not let her meet me, then she would find me on her own. The agency did not want me or my parents to be blindsided so they asked if we were open to meeting her. Therefore, at the age of 12 I met my biological mother and her family. I would in years to come have countless battles with the spirit of abandonment, due to ending up an orphan, with the curse of an abandoned spirit now attached to my life.

Abandon: To give up on completely, desert, (Webster New World Dictionary page 1)

This is what I have felt like so many times in my life. I have felt deserted, alone, and given up on completely. No matter what happens in life when a spirit attaches itself to you through your bloodline, it is a real spirit that you have to deal with and fight to overcome. This spirit of abandonment was passed down through my bloodline from my mother. Even though my biological mother had parents who raised her she still felt abandoned, when they passed away at an early age. She felt deserted and given up on. Therefore, she had me in order to try and fix her emotional problems. When that did not work she ended up feeling the same feelings of abandonment, with a much larger problem of now being a single mother and ultimately a desolate mother. She passed the same spirit to me through desertion, not by any choice of her own. Due to her emotional and mental instability, she could not adequately care for me.

Now I have been born into a world where my mother cannot care for me and has now left me abandoned with no father around. Then I ended up an orphan in an orphanage and eventually in foster care. So you see how the spirit of abandonment has been so easily passed down to me and began a fear, curse, reality that would plague me the first half of my life. There are some iniquities that a person cannot control. Iniquities are: "wickedness – ties, a wicked or unjust act. (Webster New World Dictionary page 1) It is an injustice when a soul tie and sin through no control of your own is passed down to you. However, you now have it and must figure out how to defeat it.

I admit to having the issue of abandonment at this early stage in life, and thus wanting to feel loved. As previously mentioned, this is a generational curse that my mother has passed down through her blood line. Therefore I have repeated and did a lot of drastic things in life like my mother did in order to accomplish the feeling of being loved. Things like, allowing people to treat me any kind of way, being in relationships just to have a false sense of love, being violent in the past to have a sense of control, and being overly aggressive to avoid feeling vulnerable and insecure. Thank God in 2007 while up in my prayer room I made the connection that these were my issues, and why I had these issues. I immediately began to work on myself so that I would no longer be a victim of my circumstances. I chose to become more than an overcomer!

After I became an orphan and went into the foster care system, I eventually ended up with a family who chose to adopt me. My adopted parents were always honest in telling me that I was adopted. In total my parents had eight children. Four of us were adopted including me. My adopted brother told me that the only reason my new family kept me, was because my father loved me so much. My adopted father and I were very close. He always protected me and taught me lessons in life. My mother did not like the fact that we were close.

When I was growing up I can say that I had a lot of fun as a child playing with my friends, brothers and sisters. However, there was always a part of me that felt as if I did not belong and was an outcast. I was treated differently than my siblings. For example, I was often called a disgrace by my adopted mother. She would tell me that I am going to be just like my biological mother. She would often just haul off and hit me in my head while I was washing dishes. It would come out of nowhere. I was called ugly and sometimes an ugly black Ethiopian. On weekends I had to clean way more than my siblings. They had normal chores like cleaning your room and maybe one other area of the house. In addition to my regular chores I was ordered to move all of the furniture, couches ect. and clean the baseboards. I had to take down the blinds and wash them at least every other week. Nightly, it was my job to clean the kitchen after dinner. Sometimes my mom would take every dish from the cabinets and make me wash them all over again, just because. After dinner I was required to clean the kitchen floor, tile by tile on my hands and knees. When my brother strolled in the house in the middle of the night he would make himself something to eat. My mom would snatch the covers off of me and yell at

15

me to get up and clean up his mess. She would also take all of my clothes out of my dresser and my closet and throw them on the floor just to make me put them away all over again. I cleaned so much, which is why now I cannot see having a house any other way, but clean.

I had very little clothes compared to my siblings. It seemed as though my mom would take them shopping for clothes and shoes almost every other weekend. I had to mix and match my outfits to make the best of what little I had in order to make it through the week. I remember saving a couple of dollars here and there from my part-time job so that I can buy a few pieces of clothing. I also obtained clothes through borrowing from friends or whatever other means necessary. As a teenager, I cannot ever remember going clothing shopping with my family. My older sister and I had the exact same birthday. My birthday was never acknowledged but my sister's always was. I never got a "happy birthday", cake, party, nothing. These incidents are just a fraction of what I went through as a child. We often got beatings, but that was par for the course in most black family households. Beatings are not what I saw as unfair because we all got them when we misbehaved. It was the aforementioned incidents and so much more that were isolated to only me. It was not until I got a little older that I realized I was looked at and treated somewhat differently.

When my adopted mother would tell me that I'm going to be just like my biological mother, I did not understand what she meant by those **words**. **Word**s have power, and they can come to life. Being as though my parents were the pastor and first lady of a Pentecostal church they were esteemed as the man and woman of God. They had the power through God to speak differently over my life. My adopted mother with her **word**s spoke over my life and would tell me that I am going to be just like my biological mother. She would say this to me again and again. My adopted father, must have understood the power of **word**s, so at the age of 16 he told me to move out on my own because if I did not then my adopted mother would "drive me crazy" just like my biological mother. Now I really felt like I was abandoned not only by my biological family but also by my adopted family. I was 16 years old out in the world and felt like I did not have a real family of my own to love me. I found myself in a similar situation as my biological mother when she was 15, feeling abandoned. At that time, satan tried to play with my mind and have me believe, maybe, just maybe I will be just like my biological mother. But God said not so! He knew my purpose in life. He knew my expected end. And he told me to trust him and walk with him.

I chose to believe and rely on God even through the feelings of abandonment. I knew that God had my back and would never leave me or forsake me. My adopted father asking me to leave and showing me how to bend my knees and pray are the two greatest gifts that he could have ever given me to launch me into true freedom. To me, he was the best father ever! I will always love him. When people counted me out and watched me with keen eyes wondering if I would turn out to be just like my biological mother, God said "not so"! At times folks shunned away from me and told me not to expect anything from them simply because I was adopted and then abandoned. People, friends, family, and loved ones would compare me to my biological mother even though some of them never knew her personally. Some of them only heard that she had a mental illness and would chose to compare me to her, but God said "not so"!

The hand and favor of God has always been on my life. "Surely goodness and mercy shall follow me all the days of my life: and I will dwell in the house of the Lord for ever." (Psalms 23:6) I believe in the scripture that says, "Touch not mine anointed, and do my prophets no harm." (I Chronicles 16:22) I know that I am a child of God and he has an ordained purpose for my life to share with other's his love, faithfulness, forgiveness, and promises that he has for their lives. I believe that God has always and will always cover me and protect me from demise. My God knows that I will never deny him because I know him. He has been dependable and has proven to me that he lives and he is a keeper. He is a way maker, a burden bearer, a friend, a very present help in the time of trouble. God is the beginning and the end. He is whatever I need him to be. God is an awesome God, Father and Savior. "Eye hath not seen, nor ear heard, neither have entered into the heart of man, the things which God hath prepared for them that love him." (I Corinthians 2:9) God said, stay tuned because and eyes have not seen nor have ears heard what God has in store for Michelle D. Whitmore.

17

Why, because I love God. I am honest with him about my issues. I keep working on my issues. I try not to be selfish. I help others as Christ has helped me. I rely on him for my healing, love, peace, joy, and my everything. God knows because I always let him know just how thankful I am to him. I constantly remind him that he is my everything. In him I live, move and have my being. I am nothing without God and I am not ashamed to say this. Daily, I tell him that I am grateful for everything, from having water to bathe in, food to eat, feet to walk on, the ability to smile, friends, family, a job as my resource, my beautiful daughter, knees to bend an pray, a mouth to talk and give God thanks, heat in my house, and so much more. I don't limit myself to be grateful for only big things but I express to God that I am grateful for little things as well and most importantly, everything! I am open with everyone that knows me that God is my source and everything else is my resource. I teach my child the same thing. She has a relationship with God her father. She is vocal about how thankful she is to God for everything. When she prays to God, she believes that he will give her what she asked for. My prayer for her is that God continues to protect her heart and mind and not allow her to succumb to the spirit of abandonment.

Many of you also deal with the spirit of abandonment and rejection for various reasons. You may have had a parent who was not mentally and emotionally stable such as mine or one who was addicted to drugs, alcohol, sex, money, fame ect....and left you motherless or fatherless. This can be a huge turning point in your life when you feel that you are worthless, lost, afraid and unsure of your purpose in life. But please know that you always have a father in heaven that says, "Be strong and of a good courage, fear not, nor be afraid of them: for the LORD thy God, he it is that doth go with thee; he will not fail thee, nor forsake thee." (Deuteronomy 31:6) "When my father and my mother forsake me, then the LORD will take me up." (Psalms 27:10) "For I know the thoughts that I think toward you, saith the LORD, thoughts of peace, and not of evil, to give you an expected end." (Jeremiah 29:11) "There is a friend that sticketh closer than a brother. (Proverbs 18:24) When you speak the **word** of God (bible) into your life God must honor his **word** and bring it to pass. You will see the spirit of the lord become a comforter. "I will not leave you comfortless: I will come to you." (John 14:18) God will give you joy for every tear you cry. "They that sow in tears shall reap in joy." (Psalms 126:5) He will lift your heavy burdens. "Cast thy burden upon the LORD, he shall sustain thee: he shall never suffer the righteous to be moved." (Psalms 55:22) God will give you strength to withstand tribulation. He will give you wings like eagles to fly, walk and not faint. "But they that wait upon the LORD shall renew their strength; they shall mount up with wings as eagles; they shall run, and not be weary; and they shall walk, and not faint." (Isaiah 40:31) God will cause you to travail and make your enemies your footstool. "The LORD said unto my Lord, Sit thou at my right hand, until I make thine enemies thy footstool." (Psalms 110:1) And above all, God will bring you everlasting peace. "For he is our peace." (Ephesians 2:14) His **word** brings you LIFE! His **word** walks with you! His **word** becomes a light unto your feet and a lamp unto your path. You will never feel abandoned, lost, afraid, worthless and unsure of yourself in his **word**. You are made in the image of God and he called you Good. "And God said, Let us make man in our image, after our likeness" (Genesis 1:26). "And God saw everything that he had made, and behold, it was very good." (Genesis 1:31)

Remember in the beginning of this journey I said that the hardest thing to do is look in the mirror. In order for God to step in and save us from ourselves we must be honest with him first and confess our reality/truth. Examples: God I feel abandoned. God I feel lonely. God I feel worthless. God I feel insufficient. God I am a liar. God I am a thief. God I am a gossiper. God I am a whore. God I have a bad attitude. Please help me God! Only then will God begin to help us. There are many complex sides to us that God understands. Some things are our truths (God I am) and some are LOL (lies of life) which have caused us to feel a certain way (God I feel). Sometimes when people treat us a certain, way or tell us that we are nobody, worthless, and insufficient you take that into your spirit and you believe it. You must understand that these are lies of life because your creator, God, in his **word** said that he created you in his image and likeness and called you very good! In his **word** he did not say that you were insufficient, worthless, or nobody. So, no matter what lies you have been told about yourself, you must be bold and speak the **word** of God over your life. The bible says, "let the weak say, I am strong." (Joel 3:10)

19

The bible also says, "Verily I say unto you, Whatsoever ye shall bind on earth shall be bound in heaven: and whatsoever ye shall loose on earth shall be loosed in heaven." (Matthew 18:18) So begin to bind those things about yourself that you know are true and not aligned with the **word** of God. Also, start to bind those lies that people said about you that are false and are not aligned with who God called you to be. Begin to loose what the **word** of God called you to be!

Philippians 4: 6-9

6. Be careful for nothing; but in every thing by prayer and supplication with thanksgiving let your requests be made known unto God.

7. And the peace of God which passeth all understanding, shall keep your hearts and minds through Christ Jesus.

8. Finally, brethren, whatsoever things are true, whatsoever things are honest, whatsoever things are just, whatsoever things are pure, whatsoever things are lovely, whatsoever things are of good report; if there be any virtue, and if there be any praise, think on these things.

9. Those things, which ye have both learned, and received, and heard, and seen in me do: and the God of peace shall be with you.

"I can do all things through Christ which strengtheneth me." (Phillipians 4:13)

Galatians 5: 22-23

22. But the fruit of the Spirit is love, joy, peace, longsuffering, gentleness, goodness, faith,

23. Meekness; temperance: against such there is no law.

Let's pause for a moment, close your eyes and begin to confess to God how you feel and what you are.

Now, let's quote some scriptures above and say to God, your word says that I am..... and I feel.... God, I believe that your word is true and I am asking you to take these feelings that are not in line with your word away from me and place love, joy, peace, longsuffering, gentleness, goodness, and faith inside of me in Jesus name. Amen.

Bless God!!!!!

What we have to learn in life is that before we can move forward and become successful in many areas of our lives we must deal with the character flaws that are hindering our success, joy and peace. For example, before we can land a dream job, build a successful business, parent or mentor a child we need to fix inherited spirits first. If not, we are going to take those same personality and spiritual flaws with us which will set you up for abysmal failure. And if you do not correct those defects about yourself, you will pass them on to the people, staff, children and everyone that you come in contact with. A mentor once told me that God will not take you where your character cannot keep you.

At the age of 27 I brought my first house. I built a prayer room on the 3rd floor according to priestly garments in Exodus 28. At around age 29 I spent 120 days in my prayer room sleeping on the floor confessing what I feel and who I am to God. I had to deal with the man in the mirror, and break the spirit of abandonment and rejection off of me. It took studying the **word** of God and allowing the spirit of God to discontinue the iniquities that were passed down to me in order to be completely healed. As conveyed above, these iniquities caused me to have character flaws as well. I had to pray that those impediments in life were broken off of me. I knew that if this did not change then my life would end up a disaster.

After the spirit and fear of abandonment was broken off of my life, through God's **word** and his loving spirit, I knew with certainty that I was never alone and that God would always be there for me. God will always have my back! God's desire is for us to have access to whatever we need and desire. He is here to help us. If we take one step he will take two.

I am grateful that God is a forgiving God. He will give us what we need to move forward in life and let go of the hurt from the past. After my father passed away, my adopted mother called me and asked if we can meet up. She apologized for mistreating me the way that she did and admitted that she was jealous of the close relationship that my father and I had. I forgave her. From that point forward, God created a new love within my heart for my mother because the old love that I had was destroyed by hatred and anger surrounding my ill-treatment. We became friends. I respected her for the lady that she was and for raising me. She respected me for the woman that I became. It takes work to build character and integrity. If we want to see change, we must put our work in.

Hebrew 13: 5-6

5. Let your conversation be without covetousness; and the content with such things as ye have: for he hath said, I will never leave thee, nor forsake thee.

6. So that we may boldly say, The Lord is my helper, and I will not fear what man shall do unto me.

Chapter Three

Rebellion

Rebellion: A defiance of any authority

In my teens and early twenties I did not feel loved, and I began to **rebel** and do a lot of irrational things like smoke weed, drink alcohol, fight with anyone including men. This all started around age 14. I knew these things were wrong but at the time I felt as though I did not know how to cope with the problems that I was going through which were: feeling like a bastard child, an outcast, and rejected. I didn't know how to escape the bondage that I was feeling, so I dealt with it through rebelling. I thought that I was bringing a relief to myself, while all the while I was hurting myself and others at the same time.

When I moved out of my parent's house at 16 years of age, my friends were telling me that I was foolish to leave such an aesthetically beautiful home. I moved into my Godmother's apartment and shared a bed with her for the next 2 years until l went to college. At first I sensed that there was love in my Godmother's home. I felt freedom in my mind, and a burden lifted, only for a bigger worry to be right around the corner. The liberation that I felt was only a temporary feeling. I had too much freedom for a teenager. I needed structure, and discipline along with love. So I continued to rebel, begging for structure to come in order to feel safe and guided. I would do things like stay out all weekend, smoke weed, drink and fight. Thank God I was never offered any other drugs and I had no desire to try any. I worked three jobs while in high school and hung out with drug dealers who were like brothers to me. Even though I kept rebelling, feeling lost, and wandering, the hand of God was still on me. He lovingly covered me from major hurt, harm and danger. He did not allow anything to happen to me that would further obstruct my future

Rebellion I Samuel 15:23-25 –

23. For rebellion is as the sin of witchcraft, and stubbornness is as iniquity and idolatry. Because thou hast rejected the **word** of the Lord, he hath also rejected thee from the beginning king.

24. And Saul said unto Samuel, I have sinned: for I have transgressed the commandment of the Lord, and thy **word**s: because I feared the people, and obeyed their voice.

25. Now therefore, I pray thee, pardon my sin, and turn again with me, that I may worship the Lord

This is what God does for us even though we become disobedient to his **word** and we rebel. Because he loves us he will pardon our sin and allow us freedom again to worship him. God's grace and mercy covers us even when we are rebellious because he has a purpose for our lives. Thank God for his scripture that says:

TOUCH NOT MY ANNOINTED NOR DO MY PROFIT NO HARM.

I Chronicles 16:22 – "Saying, Touch not mine anointed, and do my prophets no harm."

Chapter Four

How Storms Arise

Be careful of what information you share in sincerity and confidence with people who care about you and who you are close to, because sometimes they will turn this information against you and use it to hurt you, in hopes to watch your downfall and demise. There was a time in life when I shared with some friends about my biological mother and my upbringing. Some of them judged me. For example, let's say you went on a trip with a friend and you called them out of their name, they would rightfully get angry. However, if they did this to me and I became upset they would say I'm overreacting and acting crazy just like my biological mother. Let's also use another example where an elderly family member asked me to go grocery shopping for them because they could not trust their adult son, who had stolen from them time and time again to fund a drug habit. When I went to the house and negligently left my purse in an accessible place that same son stole from me. The elderly family member insinuated that I was crazy like my biological mother and my money was never stolen. How about a time when I had hyperemesis which is a rare condition that 0.5% of pregnant women have, only during the pregnancy. Another family member said that it was all in my head insinuating that I was crazy and overreacting just like my biological mother. When that same person had an aneurism months later I was not mean enough to say to her that it was in her head literally. I just relayed that I wished her well. How about a time where I was on a trip with my ex-fiancé, and we had an argument over a woman that he was having an affair with. He sat in my face and screamed slurs over and over again in my face that I would be just like my mother.

From my adopted mother telling me that I was going to be just like my biological mother to my friends and biological family insinuating the same thing, people don't realize that the bible says life and death are in the power of the tongue. Sometimes people fail to realize that they have power to speak life into someone or death over someone. It is satans' will that people are ignorant of what they are saying by just speaking ignorance into the atmosphere. There were times in life that I started to believe what they said I would become. I believed that they loved me and they knew me better than I knew myself. As I got older I asked God, what does all of this mean? Is this a demonic attack that satan has out for my life causing my emotions and actions to demonstrate these behaviors that were volatile? I asked God to please expose it to me and deliver me from this spirit so that I will not become that which satan has desired me to become from the beginning of my life. What I had to come to realize was that they don't know me better than God, the father, my creator who knows me best. Through these experiences I have realized that I must protect my ear gates and control what I allow to be said to me. I realized that I did not have to accept what these people have spoken over my life.

At a very young age satan had an attack against my life because of what he knew I would become. My life is based on the **word** of God that says: Before I was born and in the womb of my mother God knew me and ordained me a profit to the nations. He told me to not be afraid of their faces but to speak the **word**s that he put in my mouth. "Before I formed thee in the belly I knew thee; and before thou camest forth out of the womb I sanctified thee, and I ordained thee a prophet unto the nations." (Jeremiah 1:5) So while satan and all his workers stand around to attack my life and watch the fall of God's daughter I have news for them that says "Eyes have not seen nor ears heard"!

To this day people watch me closely to see if eventually I am going to turn into my mother. They are in disbelief that after all I have been through in my lifetime, life's experiences, along with genetics have not cracked me and caused me to be mentally ill. I am a strong woman because God keeps me. The **word** of God says: "When the enemy shall come in like a flood, the spirit of the LORD shall lift up a standard against him." (Isaiah 59:19) Therefore when I am tested and tried I run to God, my strong tower, my rock, in whom I trust.

II Samuel 22: 2-4

2. And he said, The Lord is my rock, and my fortress, and my deliverer;

3. The God of my rock; in him will I trust; he is my shield, and the horn of my salvation, my high tower, and my refuge, my savior; thou savest me from violence.

4. I will call on the Lord, who is worthy to be praised: so shall I be saved from mine enemies.

When dealing with trouble, strife, and storms in every area of my life, from work to family, raising my child and all of my responsibilities, I too get weak. It is then that I run to my refuge, my rock, my help, God my father. I know that he will give me the strength to run on and complete my journey and purpose in life.

Isaiah 40: 30-31

30. Even the youths shall faint and be weary, and the young men shall utterly fall:

31. But they that wait upon the Lord shall renew their strength; they shall mount up with wings as eagles; they shall run, and not be weary; and they shall walk, and not faint.

Psalms 24: 7-8

7. Lift up your heads, O ye gates; and be ye lift up, ye everlasting doors; and the King of glory shall come in.

8. Who is this King of glory? The LORD strong and mighty, the LORD mighty in battle.

I know that God has my back! The LORD will block the enemy's attempt to sabotage what he has planned for me. For example, this book was challenging for me to write because I wanted to help people come out of bondage and live a more powerful, purposed driven life. I desire to help folks realize their potential and individual power that God placed inside of them to make a difference in life. You have the ability to affect change, chose your path and achieve your dreams. I long to help people let go of events that happened to them in the past that causes them to be stuck and unable to move forward in life. I ache to see people delivered from bitterness, anger, fear, and hatred. These are just ploys of the enemy to convince you that you are justified in feeling this way because of what someone did to you or what happened to you. Yes, you felt that way, but let's not hold on to it. Holding on to it only negatively affects you! It keeps you in bondage! It keeps you blinded and unable to see beyond the great horizons of what your life can be. Your future can be amazing and purposeful as God intended. It can be fruitful and driven. You must start with confessing how you truly feel instead of denying it. Then you must denounce that spirit to let go of you, your children, your family and your future! Pray and battle that what happened to you does not happen to your offspring, your family, friends, neighbors, or your enemies! Tell satan that he is a liar and that he does not have any power. God has given you the power! "And I will give unto thee the keys of the kingdom of heaven: and whatsoever thou shalt bind on earth shall be bound in heaven: and whatsoever thou shalt loose on earth shall be loosed in heaven." (Matthew 16:19)

God has given me the ability to forgive. I have learned immensely that I no longer need to be in control over every aspect of my life because then I am being my anxious in my spirit by saying, God you don't have this.

"For God hath not given us the spirit of fear; but of power, and of love, and of a sound mind" (II Timothy 1:7)

Chapter Five

Ugly, Useless,

When I was young I was often told that I was Ugly. I was told that I did not fit in with my family and that I was a disgrace to the family. For many years I was insecure and felt as if I was useless and an outcast. I clearly did not fit and was treated as so. When I was born I was told that my biological name was Dru Michelle. My adopted parents renamed my first name to Michelle. I have been called "Michelle" all of my life. Again, **word**s speak life. The more you speak something into existence the more it is so, because that is how God created us to be. He created us in his image to have power in our tongue and our **word**s in order to create things and bring them to life. "Death and life are in the power of the tongue." (Proverbs 18:21) Those who told me I was ugly as a child did not realize that the more they called my name, Michelle, they were creating beauty. The definition of "Michelle" means "beautiful". The more people kept speaking my name the more they spoke my future into existence. When I was in prayer, in my 20's, I was pouring out my heart telling God about my insecurities due to me being called ugly. I asked God why did this happen to me? I heard God's voice say, they did not know what they were doing but I had them to rename you "Michelle" because it means beautiful and that is what you are, inside and out. They did not know what they were speaking into my life. The more times you say it the more times you speak it into the spirit realm and the angels watching over me caught it and begin working on that **word**. Have you ever heard the terminology actions speak louder than **word**s? Well, in God's eyes both are important?

"Even so faith, if it hath not works, is dead, being alone." (James 2:17)

"I will praise thee; for I am fearfully and wonderfully made: marvelous are thy works; and that my soul knoweth right well." (Psalms 139:14)

I Peter 3: 3-4

3. Whose adorning let it not be that outward adorning of plaiting the hair, and of wearing of gold, or of putting on of apparel:

4. But let it be the hidden man of the heart, in that which is not corruptible, even the ornament of a meek and quiet spirit, which is in the sight of God of great price.

If God gave you the ability to speak then he wants you to use that tool to worship him. If he gave you the ability to bend your knees and bow down, or clap your hands then he wants you to use that too. We as humans always limit ourselves to circumstances that don't require us to work hard or step outside of our comfort zone. God desires a sacrifice from us. He desires for us to worship him in all that we do. God desires a sacrifice of prayer and praise.

"And he humbled thee, and suffered thee to hunger, and fed thee with manna, which thou knewest not, neither did thy fathers know; that he might make thee know that man doth not live by bread only, but by every **word** that proceedeth out of the mouth of the Lord doth man live." (Deuteronomy 8:3)

"Thy **word** is a lamp unto my feet, and a light unto my path." (Psalms 119:105)

"For the **word** of God is quick, and powerful, and sharper than any twoedged sword, piercing even to the dividing asunder of soul and spirit, and of the joints and marrow, and is a discerner of the thoughts and intents of the heart." (Hebrews 4:12)

"But the **word** of the Lord endureth for ever. And this is the **word** which by the gospel is preached unto you." (I Peter 1:25)

"Heaven and earth shall pass away: but my **word**s shall not pass away." (Mark 13:31)

"If ye abide in me, and my **word**s abide in you, ye shall ask what ye will, and it shall be done unto you." (John 15:7)

You must step outside of your comfort zone and face head on those things that are attacking you causing you to shun away from your true purpose and a better you. You must challenge the **word** of God to work in your life and challenge your faith to believe. On a work out tape that I do, the instructor says "If you want to see the body change you must put pressure on it and then challenge yourself to adapt and change". The body will adapt and change. Well I challenge you to move beyond what people call you and what you have chosen to answer to. I challenge you to break all curses that satan has you bound by. I challenge you for the next thirty days to address each one of your issues. How?

If your issues are: love, pain, fear, etc.... look up these **word**s in the back of the bible in the accordance section. Read scriptures that are attached to these **word**s to see what God says about those issues. After you read the scriptures say a small prayer to God by 1st being thankful, 2nd being honest about your feelings and issues, and 3rd asking him for his help.

On the same day you can again look in the accordance and find **word**s such as: joy, peace, greatness and see what the **word** of God says about you. Begin to speak these things into your life and fill your cup with the **word** of God. After you have emptied it out and been delivered from your curses I also challenge you to read Genesis chapters 1-5.

This will be a little work on your part but you will see true change. Rise to the challenge in order to save your future and the generations after you.

Chapter Six

Free Your Mind

PTSD – is an mental illness that can develop after a person is exposed to one or more traumatic events, such as sexual assault, warfare, traffic collisions, terrorism, or other threats on a person's life. Symptoms include disturbing recurring flashbacks, avoidance or numbing of memories of the event, and hyperarousal, continue for more than a month after the occurrence of the event.

https://en.wikipedia.org/wiki/Posttraumatic_stress_disorder

Many people deal with Post Traumatic Stress Disorder. After occurrences noted above and some not mentioned such as bullying, rape, assault, divorce, miscarriage, abortion, ect., it is important to seek God for deliverance through reading the bible/**word** of God, and praying. It is also important for some to attend therapy just to talk to someone about the event and learn coping mechanisms to help you move forward in life. Many Christians denounce counseling but God has put all resources here for his people to help bring healing. God is your source and everything else is a resource.

Ever since I was young I have been double minded in my decision making. Some say it's because I am a Gemini. This may be true (laughing) "A double minded man is unstable in all his ways." (James 1:8) I can recall attributing it to the fact that I wanted to please many people at one time. Why, because I no longer wanted to deal with the feeling of rejection anymore. I felt that if I pleased everyone, then they would accept me into their family and or circles and would not reject me. Be mindful because satan will play tricks on your mind mainly to cause worry. He will have you think that someone is talking about you when they are not even thinking about you. He will cause you to have anxiety, fear, uneasiness, discomfort and apprehension to move forward in life. He will do anything to keep you stuck and ensure that you live life unhinged, insecure, erratic, and unbalanced. This is his job. When you become these things then you are not whole but broken and vulnerable. This leaves space open for him to creep in and work on destroying you. His job is to ensure that you do not evolve or advance and that you are not productive in life. His job is to ensure that you have unrest. You do not have to allow this to happen. God came to give us peace. You must start to lean on God and believe in his **word** which says….

"Thou wilt keep him in perfect peace, whose mind is stayed on thee: because he trusted in thee." (Isaiah 26:3)

"But he was wounded for our transgressions, he was bruised for our iniquities: the chastisement of our peace was upon him; and with his stripes we are healed." (Isaiah 53:5)

"For he is our Peace" (Ephesians 2:14)

"And the peace of God which passeth all understanding, shall keep your hearts and minds through Christ Jesus." (Philippians 4:7)

There are many avenues that lead to rejection. It is easier to inherit the spirit of rejection through your primary caregiver. They are the ones who are closest to you holding and caring for you daily. Now remember I told you the story about my mom and how she felt rejected, thus wanting to have me to fill that void. After giving birth, my mom did not want me because my skin was not white enough. So she cut me open in an attempt to get her white baby back. My biological family reported this to child protective services and the state took me away from her. My biological family told me stories that they wanted me and tried to get custody of me but really there is no proof that they did. My adopted mother did not want me. Can you see how God in his infinite wisdom helped my adopted father to see, that even at the tender age of 16 it was best for me to leave my house in order to save me from further damage both mentally and emotionally. God also in his never-ending wisdom knew what my future would be like if he allowed me to stay with my biological mother and allowed her to stay around to touch, handle, and fondle me. Although she was able to do this for about 6 months until the state took me away, satan was well on his way to accomplish his plan to destroy me but God snatched me out in the nick of time.

There are many curses passed down from generation to generation. These curses can produce hurt, anger, bitterness, jealousy, rejection and more. I too had generational curses passed down that I was determined would stop with me. One curse was the spirit of rejection as I demonstrated earlier. I decided to obliterate the curses which produced nothing but negativity and pain. I decided to replace these curses with good fruit. I started with asking God to help me. I told him that I refused to believe what people said about me and to limit myself to what they said I would become. I decided with the help of God, that I am going to live out my full purpose in life. It all starts with reprogramming your mind. "And be not conformed to this world: but be ye transformed by the renewing of your mind, that ye may prove what is that good, and acceptable, and perfect, will of God." (Romans 12:2) I realized that my mind can be transformed and renewed now according to the **word** of God. Daily we must renew our mind and visualize the dreams and aspirations we have. "Let this mind be in you, which was also in Christ Jesus" (Philippians 2:5) I also realized that I can do whatever I set my mind to. I keep telling myself; with God all things are possible. I decided to reprogram my mind in that manner. "With men this is impossible; but with God all things are possible." (Matthew 19:26)

You don't have to live with insecurities anymore because they too are holding you back from moving forward in life. I use an example of insecurities as a person who is in a relationship with someone that you know is not good for you, but you keep him/her around just to say that you have someone because you think that being in a relationship makes you secure. The revelation of those that deal with insecurities is like carrying a "dead" person on your back just to have someone around even if they are dead weight. Some elect to still carry this dead corpse even if you have to deal with the stench and troubles of a dead person which then begins to plague you. In your mind you may believe that it is better to have someone around then to be alone. Research shows that you cannot get a disease from touching a dead corpse unless the deceased has a contagious disease that you become exposed to through fluids. Once that dead body starts to get consumed with maggots, then bot flies which are also larvae/maggots can start to eat away at your living flesh. And if you, yourself have some dead tissue within - depression, anger, pity, un-forgiveness, ect... then those same bot flies and larvae/maggots will also begin to eat away at your dead flesh. Do you want those same maggots to be all over of you? The person in your life that you are keeping around can be reeking with odor. This dead weight that you are choosing to carry in conjunction with your own daily life burdens, are collectively causing your spirit to slowly die. You have to find the courage to let go of dead weight, people, careers, churches, and habits. Find the strength through the power and grace of God to walk away. Move forward in faith knowing that God is with you and will guide you every step of the way so long as you keep focused on him. Start by reprogramming your mind and telling yourself that God created me to be better than this. I must heal myself first so that I can be whole and get my life back. Once you start living again then surround yourself with other living people who are doing something and focused driven. It is necessary, selfless, and Godly to reach back and help others up. However, you must remember that you are reaching back in strength to help them up. Do not allow them to drag you back down. Don't straddle the fence, become doubleminded, and accidentally get pulled back down. Reach and pull! You can do this! Your help comes from God!

Psalms 121: 1-2

1. I will lift up mine eyes unto the hills, from whence cometh my help

2. My help cometh from the LORD, which made heaven and earth.

3. He will not suffer thy foot to be moved:

One very bad double mindedness decision I made was to have an abortion in the past. The man that I was with was cheating on me with another woman. At the time I felt that I did not want my child to be fatherless. Somewhere deep down inside of me, I felt that if I had my child I would pass down the generational curse of feeling rejected and abandoned to my kid. I could not live with the thought of my child feeling abandoned so therefore I aborted hoping and praying that God would find it in his heart to smile on me and help me break the generational curse. Well clearly, when many of us make decisions out of our emotions we make some of the worst decisions ever. Having that abortion for the reasons that I did was absolutely one of my worst decisions. The abortion definitely did not break the generational curse of rejection and abandonment. Only God had the power to break that off of me! I also considered aborting my daughter that is present today. I did not want her to feel abandoned or rejected. At the time that I was pregnant, I came down with a rare condition called hyperemesis. It affects your system and causes you to vomit all day long with no relief in sight. This can go on for three months all the way until you give birth. It causes extreme weight loss and dehydration. My condition lasted until I was about 6 months pregnant. I went from being with her father at least six days a week when we were dating to not seeing him at all when I reached about 8 weeks pregnant. I knew something was up, but I didn't know exactly what it was. It was not until after my daughter was born at 3 months old that I found out he was actively married. When her father went AWOL during my first trimester this is when I considered aborting. I did not want my child to feel rejected and abandoned because I knew what a lasting scar these decisions in life could cause.

I don't wish hyperemesis on my worst enemy. However, to this day, I thank God for having that condition because it caused me to be so sick that I could not move my body and get up, even if my desire was to get an abortion. Hyperemesis had debilitated me to the degree where I could not make any decisions or care for myself. I believe that this was God's way of saying, enough is enough! The curse will not be broken by me trying to control the situation and abort the child. The curse will only be broken when I cry loud, and ask God to forgive me, and face the issue head on! I had to pray and continue to pray that my daughter will not be plagued with this curse. I had to first start with breaking the curse off of me! I no longer feel abandoned or rejected due to my circumstances in life while growing up. Dealing with these issues in life is not a one-time fix. You must continue to walk in your deliverance. You must continue to deal with your issues and get delivered again and again and again. This comes with continually praying; emptying yourself out and filling yourself back up with the **word** of God. I also, do the same thing with my daughter. I first speak the truth to her. When she asks me where her father is, I always tell her the truth. Then I pray over her with fervor while she is crying and emptying herself out and dealing with the realities of her situation. I then speak the **word** of God back into her vessel/her life. I read to her and tell her what the **word** of God says about her. I tell her what her father in heaven says about her. I tell her how much she is loved by her extended family that God gave her here on earth. And periodically I also take her to therapy. This brings her healing. Again, this will not be a one-time fix. This process of walking in healing, peace, love, faith, hope, and so much more is just that. It is a process and it comes with work. My daughter is a believer and loves the LORD. She recognized that he is "I am, that I am" whatever she needs him to be. She knows that she is loved. For her, for myself and for millions of people out there I strive to be whole so that I can help them be whole.

When we try to fix things ourselves like Adam and Eve in the garden tried to fix their nakedness we make a mess of things. God is the only one who can clean up our sins and cover our iniquities with his blood. I knew that if I could just be made spiritually whole then I can produce a whole righteous generation, who would be an unstoppable force, vessel and tool for the kingdom of God. I am not promoting abortion, it is wrong and I was wrong. I asked God to forgive me, but my thinking at the time goes to show you how unstable and doubleminded my thought process was. I did not realize that God's blood covers a multitude of sins and has the ability to cover my child.

"For the Lord will pass through to smite the Egyptians; and when he seeth the blood upon the lintel, and on the two side posts, the Lord will pass over the door, and will not suffer the destroyer to come in unto your houses to smite you." (Exodus 12:23)

"But if we walk in the light, as he is in the light, we have fellowship one with another, and the blood of Jesus Christ his Son cleanseth us from all sin." (I John 1:7)

"In Whom we have redemption through his blood, the forgiveness of sins, according to the riches of his grace." (Ephesians 1:7)

"A father of the fatherless, and a judge of the widows, is God in his holy habitation." (Psalms 68:5)

"When my father and my mother forsake me, then the LORD will take me up." (Psalms 27:10)

"Before I formed thee in the belly I knew thee; and before thou camest forth out of the womb I sanctified thee and I ordained thee a prophet unto the nations." (Jeremiah 1:5)

This is what God said to me before my daughter was born. She is ordained to be great! Before she was born, I always had a fear of bringing a child into this world. I was fearful that I would not be able to take care of my child, or have end up having a misfortune that would cause me to also abandon my child. The thought of my child feeling deserted was something I never wanted. I made poor choices over the course of my life and chose not to have a child until I was 32. I knew that although I was going to be alone in this journey, I had the strength and courage to "Train up a child in the way he should go: and when he is old, he will not depart from it." (Proverbs 22:6) I have an amazing daughter who is a blessing! Years ago I was reading a TD Jakes book, The Lady, Her Lover, and Her Lord. In this book TD Jakes spent a few pages talking about Chayil and the meaning of Chayil. It was so special to me that when I gave birth I named my daughter Chayil. (Woman of excellence: Thoroughbred, Graceful and Strong. A creature of Rare Beauty. An Absolute Ten. She is a Winner. Full of Strength and Wisdom. She has the force of an Army! A Diamond that has started as coal but turned into a Jewel. She is rich in Class as white wine, served in a chilled gold-stemmed goblet whirled around then sniffed before tasting. She is an Exquisite Wonder that this generation seldom beholds. She is simply a Lady. A Star. This Lady is an Endangered Species. CHAYIL is what God calls a Woman that has her Act Together. The Epitome of Defining Christian Virtue in Feminine Form. This woman is Progressive, Resourceful, Incredibly Balanced, Unique & Valuable. She is a Sensitive, Temperate, Competent Woman who has Ambitions yet possesses Finesse. A Woman of Virtue!) She is CHAYIL! This is what I believe God called my daughter to be. An awesome woman of God. I believe that God prepared me to raise her to be a whole woman years before I had her. First, by breaking off spirits from my life that would be a hindrance to both her success and my success of raising her.   Then God placed awesome **word** inside of me, to guide me through the process of raising her. I have a great purpose ahead and so does Chayil.

This journey of brining my child into the world reminded me yet again, that I no longer needed to be in control over every aspect of my life. I learned I cannot go back in time and change things so I must let go of painful situations that occurred in the past. If I remained anxious or paranoid in my spirit then, I am subconsciously saying, God you don't have this under control. You too must also learn that in your mind and heart you have to let go of negative things from the past because it is only hurting you. It is stifling you from growing and prospering. You must move on towards the plan that God has for you. You must begin to walk in the manifestation of healing and the glory of God. God has a master plan for our lives. Sometimes we get off track, but when we get back on track God will show us his glory, his hand and if you stay close enough to him, his face. My daughter and I are blessed. God has truly showed us his glory!

Galatians 4: 1-7

1. NOW I say, That the heir, as long as he is a child, differeth nothing from a servant, though he be lord of all;

2. But is under tutors and governors under tutors and governors until the time appointed of the father.

3. Even so we when we were children, were in bondage under the elements of the world:

4. But when the fullness of the time was come, God sent forth his Son, made of a woman, made under the law,

5. To redeem them that were under the law, that we might receive the adoption of some.

6. And because ye are sons, God hath sent forth the Spirit of his Son into your hearts, crying Abba, Father.

7. Wherefore thou art no more a servant, but a son: and if a son, then an heir of God through Christ.

Romans 8: 17-18

17. And if children, then heirs; heirs of God, and joint-heirs with Christ; if so be that we suffer with him, that we may be also glorified together.

18. For I reckon that the sufferings of this present time are not worthy to be compared with the glory which shall be revealed in us.

Know that God's got you! Psalms 91

1. HE THAT dwelleth in the secret place of the most High shall abide under the shadow of the Almighty.

2. I will say of the LORD, He is my refuge and my fortress: my God; in him will I trust.

3. Surely he shall deliver thee from the snare of the fowler, and from the noisome pestilence.

4. He shall cover thee with his feathers, and under his wings shalt thou trust: his wings shalt thou trust: his truth shall be thy shield and buckler.

5. Thou shalt not be afraid for the terror by night; nor for the arrow that flieth by day;

6. Nor for the pestilence that walketh in darkness; nor for the destruction that wasteth at noonday.

7. A thousand shall fall at thy side, and ten thousand at thy right hand; but it shall not come nigh thee.

8. Only with thine eyes shalt thou behold and see the reward of the wicked.

9. Because thou hast made the LORD, which is my refuge, even the most High, thy habitation;

10. There shall no evil befall thee, neither shall any plague come nigh thy dwelling.

11. For he shall give his angels charge over thee, to keep thee in all thy ways.

12. They shall bear thee up in their hands, lest thou dash thy foot against a stone.

13. Thou shalt tread upon the lion and adder: the young lion and the dragon shalt thou trample under feet.

14. Because he hath set his love upon me, therefore will I deliver him: I will set him on high, because he hath known my name.

15. He shall call upon me, and I will answer him: I will be with him in trouble; I will deliver him, and honour him.

16. With long life will I satisfy him, and show him my salvation.

Chapter Seven

HEALER!

On October 7th, 2007 I wrote in my prayer journal: "Today is October 7th 2007. Today is the day that realized I need a complete healing from the failures of my past and the fears of my future." I read Psalms 51

1. HAVE MERCY upon me, O God, according to thy lovingkindness: according unto the multitude of thy tender mercies blot out my transgressions.

2. Wash me thoroughly from mine iniquity, and cleanse me from my sin.

3. For I acknowledge my transgressions: and my sin ever before me.

4. Against thee, thee only have I sinned, and done this evil in thy sight: that thou mightest be justified when thou speakest, and be clear when thou judgest.

5. Behold, I was shapen in iniquity; and in sin did my mother conceive me.

6. Behold thou desirest truth in the inward parts: and in the hidden part thou shalt make me to know wisdom.

7. Purge me with hyssop, and I shall be clean: wash me, and I shall be whiter than snow.

8. Make me to hear joy and gladness; that the bones which thou hast broken may rejoice.

9. Hide thy face from my sins, and blot out all mine iniquities

10. Create in me a clean heart, O God; and renew a right spirit within me.

11. Cast me now away from thy presence; and take not thy holy spirit from me.

12. Restore unto me the joy of thy salvation: and uphold me with thy free spirit.

13. Then will I teach transgressors thy ways; and sinners shall be converted unto thee.

14. Deliver me from blood-guitliness, O God, thou God of my salvation: am my tounge shall sing aloud of thy righteousness

15. O Lord, open thou my lips: and my mouth shall show forth thy praise.

16. For thou desirest not sacrifice; else would I give it: thou delightest not in burnt offering.

17. The sacrifices of God are a broken spirit: a broken and a contrite heart, O God, thou wilt not despise.

18. Do good in thy good pleasure unto Zion: build thou the walls of Jerusalem.

19. Then shalt thou be pleased with the sacrifices of righteousness, with burnt offering and whole burnt offering: then shall they offer bullocks upon thine altar.

Realizing that I needed to pray the prayer of repentance I spoke out loud the entire Psalms 51. At times I shouted and cried out loud. You must start by stating what your honest issues are. Then you must ask God to deal with those issues within and wash you so that you may be clean and free. Free to worship. Free to love. Free to forgive. Free to hope. Free to trust. Free to believe. What I first realized is that truth has to ascend in order for truth to descend. No matter how many times people tell me to speak faith, I must first speak truth such as....."I am depressed. I am lonely. I am tired. I am scared. Then I can speak.... In JESUS name I am whole. I am free. I am filled. I am strong. I am courageous!

Take a moment and profess to God what you feel, and what you need to be delivered from. It is important to be honest so that you can get true healing.

Now that we have confessed the truth of what we sometimes feel and who we truthfully are, we can go to scripture as we discussed earlier in this book and find the help for our troublesome ways.

God you are the truth, and truth is a spirit, please put this spirit deep down inside of me, so in my repentance I tell the truth. I believe in your **word** that says, "Jesus said unto him, I am the way, the truth, and the life: no man cometh unto the Father, but by me." (John 14:6) All 3 are what and who I need from God to lead me down the right path to my God given destiny. I need truth in my life so that I am not wasting each precious moment with worry and heartache that is slowly killing me. I need Jesus to rise up within me and make intercession to the father for me and for my situations. So today I live in reality and I petition to God the father only the truth, so that God can descend truth.

I know at times life seems really challenging but if you can overcome these challenges then it will only make you stronger. The bible says: "For whom the Lord loveth he chasteneth." (Hebrews 12:6) As a father scolds his own child, God disciplines us because he is our father and cares about our future. He also cares about your character both throughout the journey and when you arrive to your destined purpose in life. It will not always be easy. You will be tested and put through the fire. Just know that God's desire is that you come out like pure gold and become the better for it. Work on cleaning out yourself and setting up space for God to dwell in you, lead you and guide you throughout your life.

God operates in order not confusion. You will not be able to hear God speak to you until you move all disruptions out of the way. The only way to set up the inhabitance of God within your spirit is to war in your spirit and empty yourself from all distractions and curses that have plagued you. You must then fill yourself up with the **word** of God. How? By praying and reading the **word** of God. At times you must also fast. The bible says "This kind can come forth by nothing, but by prayer and fasting." (Mark 9:29) This deliverance will come with work, but it's worth fighting for. Fighting for your relationship with God will help you to drown out all of the naysayers, failures, and setbacks of the past, and position you to hear the voice of God and his instruction for your life. When God inhabits inside of you he can begin to speak to you and step by step guide you to reach your purpose. You will then flourish and grow in leaps and bounds with the wind of the Holy Spirit pushing you into destiny. The Holy Spirit speaks to you to give you instructions.

"He that hath an ear, let him hear what the spirit saith unto the churches." (Revelation 2:29)

"Likewise the Spirit also helpeth our infirmities: for we know not what we should pray for as we ought: but the Spirit itself maketh intercession for us with groanings which cannot be uttered." (Romans 8:26)

"And he that searcheth the hearts knoweth what is the mind of the Spirit, because he maketh intercession for the saints according to the will of God." (Romans 8:27)

"God is a Spirit: and they that worship him must worship him in spirit and in truth:" (John 4:24)

"But the Comforter which is the Holy Ghost, whom the Father will send in my name, he shall teach you all things, and ring all things to your remembrance, whatsoever I have said unto you." (John 14:26)

Allow God to lead you because he loves you and wants the best for you! The Holy Spirit is here to convict the unbeliever not condemn them. He is also here for the unbeliever in order to be born again.

John 3:16-17

16. For God so loved the world, that he gave his only begotten Son, that whosoever believeth in him should not perish, but have everlasting life.

17. For God sent not his son into the world to condemn the world; but that the world through him might be saved.

You must not be afraid to expose your sins, iniquities, and nastiness, to God your father. He loves you no matter what, even though satan tries to make us afraid so that we remain ashamed, stuck and bound in order to not receive deliverance.

Fear - The moment doubt enters anything, so does death. Fear brings death. Fear brings torment.

FEAR = FALSE EVIDENCE THAT APPEARS REAL

Together, let's review some scriptures that God gave us to cast down the spirit of fear.

"For God has not given us the spirit of fear; but of power and of love, and of a sound mind." (II Timothy 1:7)

Acts 2: 25-26

25. For David speaketh concerning him, I foresaw the Lord always before my face, for he is on my right hand, that I should not be moved:

26. Therefore did my heart rejoice, and my tongue was glad; moreover also my flesh shall rest in hope:

Let me end this chapter with the story of a blind man:

John 9: 1-11, 18-25

1. AND AS Jesus passed by, he saw a man which was blind from his birth.

2. And his disciples asked him, saying, Master, who did sin, this man, or his parents, that he was born blind?

3. Jesus answered, Neither hath this man sinned, nor his parents: but that the works of God should be made manifest in him.

6. When he had thus spoken, he spat on the ground, and made clay of the spittle, and he anointed the eyes of the blind man with the clay,

7. And said unto him, Go, wash in the pool of Siloam, (which is by interpretation, sent.) He went his way therefore, and washed, and came seeing.

8. The neighbours therefore, and they which before had seen him that he was blind, said, Is not this he that sat and begged?

9. Some said, This is he: others said, He is like him: but he said, I am he.

10. Therefore said they unto him, How were thine eyes opened?

11. He answered and said, A man that is called Jesus made clay, that is called Jesus made clay, and anointed mine eyes, and said unto me, Go to the pool of Siloam, and wash: and I went and washed, and I received sight.

18. But the Jews did not believed concerning him, that he had been blind, and received his sight, until they called the parents of him that had received his sight.

19. And they asked them, saying Is this your son, who ye say was born blind? How then doth he now see?

20. His parents answered them and said, We know that this is our son, and that he was born blind:

21. But by what means he now seeth, we know not; or who hath opened his eyes, we know not: he is of age; ask him: he shall speak for himself.

24. Then again called they the man that was blind, and said unto him, Give God he praise: we know that this man is a sinner.

25. He answered and said, Whether he be a sinner or no, I know not: one thing I know, that, whereas I was blind, now I see.

What we learn here is that in verse 6 Jesus spit on the ground and made clay. He then put the clay/mud on the eyes of the blind man. In verse 7 he said to the blind man to go and wash in the pool of "sent". Although this seems unconventional, God gave this blind man a **word**/instructions which was to go and wash. The man followed God's instructions. He was then healed and could now see. There were many unbelievers who questioned whether Jesus was a sinner. The blind man spoke and said, "I don't know if he is a sinner or not, but one thing I do know was that I was blind and now I can see!"

What am I trying to say is; there comes a point in life when you are sick and tired of going through the same thing again and again and living in a mess. Life has just exhausted you with all of the drama and troubles that it brings. There are many days where you say to yourself that I don't know how to get out of these situations. There are other days where you feel like you are living in misery and torment. I am challenging you to be like the blind man. Take a leap out on faith and listen to the instructions of your creator. Lean on him to heal you and get you out of this mess. Lean on him to give you direction and bring some peace and change for the better. Don't worry about what people say. Be like the blind man and say, I don't know or care about what you think about Jesus...... all I know was that I was in bondage and now I'm free! All I know was that I was sick and now I am healed! All I know was that I was lost and now I am found! Permit God to heal you not only from sickness and disease but also from emotional and mental trauma as well.

Part Two

What does God say?

Chapter Eight

Who Is God The Savior?

"In the beginning was the <u>word</u> and the <u>word</u> was with God, and the <u>word</u> was <u>God</u>. Genesis 1:1

Let's take a look at God in the Old Testament.

II Kings 3: 11-12

> 11. But Jehoshaphat said, Is there not here a prophet of the LORD, that we may inquire of the LORD by him? And one of the king of Isreal's servants answered and said, Here is Elisha the son of Shaphat, which poured water on the hands of Elijah.

> 12. And Jehoshaphat said, the **Word** of the Lord is with him.

II Chronicles 20: 3-4

> 3. And Jehoshaphat feared, and set himself to seek the LORD, and proclaimed a fast throughout all of Judah.

4.   And Judah gathered themselves together, to ask help of the LORD:
even out of all the cities of Judah they came to seek the LORD.

II Chronicles 20:20

20. Believe in the LORD your God, so shall ye be established; believe
his prophets, so shall ye prosper.

II Chronicles 20:30

30. So the realm of Jehoshaphat was quiet: for his God gave him rest
round about.

Let's look at some excerpts from the story of Jehoshaphat. When
he feared that his people were in trouble he went to the source of what he
knew. He asked for a prophet who had a **word** from the Lord. He knew
that some things come through prayer and fasting. He also knew that if he
asked God for help, God would deliver them. God would give them a
foundation, rest, and prosperity.

I Samuel 17: 39-40

39. And David girded his sword upon his armour, and he assayed to go;
for he had not proved it. And David said unto Saul, I cannot go with
these; for I have not proved them. And David put them off him.

40. And he took his staff in his hand, and chose him five smooth
stones out of the brook, and put them in a shepherd's bag which he
had, even in a scrip; and his sling was in his hand: and he drew near to
the Philistine.

I Samuel 17:49

49: And David put his hand in his bag, and took thence a stone, and
slang it, and smote the Philistine in his forehead, that the stone sunk
into his forehead; and he fell upon his face to the earth.

David was young. He wanted to go to war and help defeat the enemy. He was permitted to go, but decided not to take a sword with him because he didn't have any proven experience using a sword when he killed animals in the wilderness. David recalls always being successful using a sling and a rock when he killed lions and bears. Therefore, he used what he knew was proven to work to defeat the enemy.

When you are desperate and in a battle for your life, there is no time for a calculated risk. You must rely on what you have experience with that has proven to work. If you ever cried out Oh God, before a car accident and you were saved then clearly you knew what to scream out! You must now acknowledge that God helped you. When you get into trouble you pray and ask God to help you. Your faith is hoping that he will answer you. We as Christians know that when we need God to answer us all we are looking for is a **word**. Just like Jehoshaphat many of us who are smart do not want to move without a **word** from God so we ask God for instructions. God must speak by his **word**s to give us an instruction. Then we must exercise our faith like Jehoshaphat and boldly stand on the **word** of God and watch him show forth his power and glory to display that his **word** is all good. We must follow God's instructions and be obedient to him. God then moves (actions). "Without faith it is impossible to please him: for he that cometh to God must believe that he is, and that he is a rewarder of them that diligently seek him." (Hebrews 11:6) He must be pleased to move. Would you grant your child something every time they asked when they continuously disobey you? <u>Probably not</u>. God is the same way. He needs to test our faith to see if we will follow his instructions before he blesses us with what we want. Just like a parent, God wants help us mature to be the best us we can be, so that we have the resolve to reach our purpose and possess the character to keep us when we get there.

It is imperative for us to understand that God works with both actions and **word**s. This is why the first step in this process is so important which is the **word**s spoken from God. How can you hear God if you are not sure what his voice sounds like? For example, if I was blindfolded and asked to identify a friend who I spoke to every day through a lineup of people speaking only a couple of **word**s, don't you think that I would choose the correct friend simply by their voice? This is how we ought to be with God.

God wants to get the glory out of our relationship with him. When tests come up, and people ask you, where is your God now? You must be able to inquire of him like David and get a couple of **word**s of instructions. Then out of that instruction be like Jehoshaphat and stand back and watch the salvation/glory of the Lord arise in the midst of whatever the situation/battle. The manifestation of God's glory and his works is what draws non-believers by the multitudes. This journey will begin to change how you think things through before making decisions. It will guide you to make the right decisions that will pay off in life to lead you to your God appointed destiny and purpose. I hope that you are starting to understand the power that you have to exercise through the **word** of God.

First, I need you to understand something about your creator before we can move forward and continue to get delivered from some things. So please read each scripture carefully.

Theme Scripture: "In the beginning was the **word** and the **word** was with **God**, and the **word** was **God**." John 1:1. Together we will breakdown this scripture and obtain a revelation, so stick with me……..In the beginning was the **word** (the actual language/speech spoken by God), and the **word** was with God.

1. The first underlined **word** above translated from the English dictionary (noun) a unit of language consisting of one or more spoken sounds or their written representation, which functions as a *principal carrier of* meaning. – God created language. God thought of something and then spoke it into existence.

2. The second underlined **word** above translated from the English dictionary (noun) A single distinct *meaningful element* of speech or writing, used with others (or sometimes alone)to form a sentence

57

3. The third underlined **word** above translated from the English dictionary (verb), choose or use particular **word**s in order to write or say something. A command, direction, order, verbal signal, *promise of assurance*.

This is similar to your biological child being part of you and without your egg or sperm creating that child there would be no child. In the beginning was the sperm (*the principal carrier of…*) and the sperm (*meaningful element*) were with Mr. xyz and the child (*promise of assurance*) was Mr. xyz's.

God created **word** and without his **word**s there would be no other creation of anything. Let me give you a clear example of what I am attempting to highlight.

This simply means that in Genesis 1:1 1-4 **"In The Beginning Was The Word"**

1. In THE beginning **God** <u>created</u> the heaven and the earth.
2. And the earth was without form, and void: and darkness was upon the face of the deep. And the spirit of **God** moved upon the face of the waters.
3. And **God** said, Let there be light: and there was light
4. And **God** saw the light, that it was good: and **God** divided the light from the darkness.

Therefore in the beginning, **God** "created" the heaven and the earth, and **God** "said" Let there be light. So you see, **God** creates, and then speaks things into existence just by his **word**s and it becomes so.

Then later on in Genesis chapter 1:26 – 27: It says **"And The Word Was With God"**

26. And **God** "said", Let us make man in our image, after our likeness: and let them have dominion over the fish of the sea, and over the fowl of the air, and over the cattle, and over all the earth, and over every creeping thing that creepeth upon the earth.

27. So **God** created man in his own image, in the image of **God** created he him, male and female created he them.

So let's refer back to our theme scripture. "In the beginning was the **Word** and the **Word** was with God and the **Word** was God." John 1:1. Every time God says something that IS his "**word**". Anytime **word**s come from the breath/vocal cords of God the **word**s are with God. Then the **word**s leave his breath to go do what he said, which demonstrates that the manifestation of God's **word** is equivalent to God. And the **word** was God. God = his **word**. Now let's simplify this. From the beginning of time, God spoke a **word**. The **word** was with God because they come from him. The breath of God and his **word**s come as an inseparable package. The **word**s that God speaks rest with the fact that these **word**s of God are God himself. Therefore the **word** of God is God and God is and rests inside of his **word**. How do we know that this does not remain alone in the past tense, because the **word** of God says: "Jesus Christ the same yesterday, and today, and forever." (Hebrews 13:8)

This is why people will say, I need a **word** from God because they know that if they get a **word** from God, they are getting God himself. And God will ensure that his **word** will achieve what he sent it to do. God will never fail! "God is not a man, that he should lie; neither the son of man, that he should repent; hath he said, and shall he not do it? Or hath he spoken, and shall he not make it good?" Numbers 23:19

Further down in Genesis chapter 1:31 it says…
31. And God saw everything that he made, and, behold, it was very good."

Therefore, if you understand and believe the **Word of God** which says that God created the wonders of the heaven and earth spoke it into existence by his **word**s alone and called it good, then surely you believe that God created you. In Genesis 1:27 he spoke you into existence by his **word**s and called you good. Not only are you a wonder, but in the **word** of

God, God said that he made you in his image. How much more of a wonder can you get than that?

We must begin to acknowledge that we were made in the image of God our creator. When he made us he called us good. And if we were made in his image then we have the power within to execute the awesome wonders of God. We too have the power to speak a **word**, know that the **word** is with God, and know that he will back up his **word** and send it to accomplish what he said. God desires to have us exercise our faith so that people will see the manifestation of his power through his **word** and come to Christ. We have the ability to change the course of our lives by what we speak, all so God can get the glory. You must begin to strengthen your faith and have confidence in who your savior is. Start by getting to know who he is, all of his attributes, and splendor.

1. "Looking unto Jesus the <u>author</u> and <u>finisher</u> of our faith" (Hebrew 12:2)
2. "And his name shall be called <u>Wonderful</u>, <u>Counsellor</u>, the <u>mighty God</u>, The <u>everlasting Father</u>, The <u>Prince of Peace</u>." (Isaiah 9:6)
3. "Thou art <u>Christ</u>, the <u>son of the living God</u>" (Matthew 16:16)
4. "Fear thou not; for I am with thee: be not dismayed: for I am thy <u>God</u>: I will strengthen thee: yea, I will help thee; yea, I will uphold thee with the right hand of my righteousness." (Isaiah 41:10)
5. "<u>Emmanuel, God with us</u>" (Matthew 1:23)
6. "The Lord is my <u>rock</u>, and my <u>fortress</u>, and my <u>deliverer</u>; my <u>God</u> my <u>strength</u>. In whom will I trust; my <u>buckler</u>, and the <u>horn of my salvation</u>, and my <u>high tower</u>." (Psalms 18:2)
7. "I am the <u>first</u>, and I am the <u>last</u>; and beside me there is no God." (Isaiah 44:6)
8. "<u>Christ in you</u>, the <u>hope of glory</u>" (Colossians 1:27)
9. "<u>Holy, holy holy</u>, <u>Lord God Almighty</u>, which <u>was</u>, and <u>is</u>, and <u>is to come</u>." (Revelation 4:8)
10. "I am the <u>Almighty God</u>." (Genesis 17:1)

11. Jehovah
    a. Jireh = my provider (Genesis 22:14)
    b. Nissi = The Lord our banner/refuge (Exodus 17:15)
    c. Tzidkaynu = The Lord our righteousness (Jeremiah 23:6)
    d. Rapha = The Lord that Heals (Exodus 15:26)
    e. Shalom – The Lord is my Peace (Judges 6: 23-24)
12. "KING of KINGS LORD of LORDS" (Revelation 19:16)
13. "Brought as Lamb to the slaughter" (Isaiah 53:7)
14. "STAND FAST therefore in the Liberty wherein Christ has made us free, and be not entangled again with the yoke of bondage" (Galatians 5:1)
15. "Ye call me Master and Lord: and ye say well: for so I am" (John 13:13)
16. "The Lord is my shepherd; I shall not want." (Psalms 23:1)
17. "Ah, Sovereign LORD, you have made the heavens and the earth by your great power and outstretched arm. Nothing is too hard for you." (Jeremiah 32:17)
18. "For he is our peace" (Ephesians 2:14)
19. "Jesus said unto her, I am the resurrection and the life. He that believeth in me, though he were dead, yet shall he live:" (John 11:25)
20. "For unto you is born this day in the city of David a Savior, which is Christ the Lord." (Luke 2:11)
21. "Jesus said unto him, that I am the way, the truth, and the life: no man cometh unto the father but by me." (John 14:6)
22. "I am the true vine, and my father is the husbandman:" (John 15:1)
23. "Worthy is the Lamb that was slain to receive power" (Revelation 5:12)
24. "And she shall bring forth a son, and thou shalt call his name JESUS for he shall save his people from their sins." (Matthew 1:21)
25. "I AM THAT I AM:" (Exodus 3:14)

These scriptures above are only a brief description of who God is. They introduce Jesus the son of **God**, born of the Virgin Mary. Emanuel interpreted **God** with us. "God is a spirit and they that worship him must worship him in spirit and in truth." (John 4:24). If you believe that God lives through man by a spirit then you believe and understand the Trinity of God the <u>father</u>, **God** the <u>son</u>, and **God** the <u>Holy Spirit</u>. The son of God is Jesus and we can pray through the Holy Spirit, in Jesus name, to make intercession for us to God. If God can do all of these amazing things with Jesus through God's spirit alone imagine what he can do with us.

Let's review the scripture below that tells us how our spirit is connected with God, through Jesus.

Romans 8: 13-17

13. For if ye live after the flesh ye shall die: but if ye through the spirit do mortify the deeds of the body, ye shall live.

14. For as many as are led by the Spirit of God they are the sons of God.

15. For ye have not received the Spirit of bondage again to fear; but ye have received the spirit of adoption, whereby we cry, Abba, Father.

16. The Spirit itself beareth witness with our Spirit, that we are the children of God.

17. And if children, then heir; heirs of God, and joint-heirs with Christ; if so be that we suffer with him that we may be also glorified together.

Here the **word** of God is telling us that if we are led by the spirit of God then we are the children of God. And if children of God then we are his heirs and joint-heirs with Jesus Christ his son. Therefore we have a right to everything that Jesus has a right to, including, "God with us" Emanuel – The **word** with us.

"God is not a man, that he should lie; neither the son of man, that he should repent; hat he said, and shall he not do it? Or hath he spoken, and shall he not make it good?" (Numbers 23:19)

So now you understand God, your creator, made you in his image. He made you an heir of God and joint heir with Jesus. You also understand that God is his **word** and whatever God has spoken in his **word** concerning you is all that matters, not what others think, or say about you. And if God and his **word** live in you through this spirit, then you carry God the Father, his son Jesus, and, the Holy Spirit inside of you. You now have access to power through our God because he is the same yesterday, today and forever. You can now speak a **word**, exercise your faith and it shall be so.

Now that we understand how we are connected with God, first by creation through his **word**, then through the breath of his spirit, we must begin to understand what the **word**, God the Father, the one who created us says about our destiny and purpose in life. Let's find out together….

We discussed this scripture earlier on in this book that God is not a man that he should lie. If he spoke the **word** then it shall come to pass. Speaking a **word** so long as you have the spirit of God within you is the divine order that God intended. "Man shall not live by bread alone, but by every **word** that proceedeth out of the mouth of God." (Matthew 4:4) This is what God intended. He desires for us to live by his **word**. We must inquire of God and get our directives from him. His **word** will restore and renew. God will be the wind beneath the wings of his **word**. You will begin to live an abundant life as God planned. God wants to breathe life back into you today so that you may begin to live again!

Chapter Nine

A Lifestyle of Ministry

Ministry – What is a life of ministry? It is: A man or woman putting themselves on the front line exhibiting love and abundance. This is what we need in order to minster the life of Jesus as our father, provider, peace, and healer.

The hardest thing to do is face the man in the mirror and make a change. Thank God that he has given us a path to do just that. The path starts with acknowledging our flaws and sins to begin the journey of living your life as the best you possible. We all have the responsibility to have a life of ministry no matter what your purpose is. If you are a doctor, a trash collector, basketball player, scientist, housewife or social services worker you have the responsibility to help others. I have found that my ministry is to help others just in my day to day or week to week interactions with people. Everything I do has purpose in order to help people out of bondage and leave a legacy behind that will continue to bring spiritual, emotional and mental freedom.

Isaiah 61: 1-3

1. The SPIRIT of the Lord GOD is upon me: because the LORD hath anointed me to preach good tidings unto the meek; he hath sent me to bind up the brokenhearted, to proclaim liberty to the captives, and the opening of the prison to them that are bound;

2. To proclaim the acceptable year of the LORD, and the day of vengeance of our God; to comfort all that mourn;

3. To appoint unto them that mourn in Zion, to give unto them beauty for ashes, the oil of joy for mourning, the garment of praise for the spirit of heaviness; that they might be the planting of the LORD, that he might be glorified.

THIS IS MY MINISTRY!

The **word** of God says "For **God** so loved the world that he gave his only begotten son, that whosoever believeth in him should not perish, but have everlasting life" (John 3:16)

If you believe that God's son, Jesus, who is bone of God's bone, flesh of his flesh, and the spirit of intercession through the Holy Ghost, then you believe that Jesus, God's only begotten son gave his life as a sacrifice for all humans so that we might be saved. You also believe and understand that Jesus is the only worthy and acceptable "lamb slain" to make intercession to the Father, God on our behalf, therefore this is why Jesus said, "I am the way, the truth, and the life, no man cometh unto the Father, but by me." (John 14:6)

"Ask, and it shall be given you; seek, and y shall find; knock, and it shall be opened unto you:" (Matthew 7:7)

Just say YES!......................Membership has its privileges

Chapter Ten

I Am His Child. I Have Rights!
I Have Power!

What society thought I would become, God said no! That is not who I created her/Michelle D. Whitmore to be. I live my life through the **word** of God. I realize that I am his child and I have rights. I believe that his **word** will not return unto him void. So when I am dealing with an issue, crisis, situation or simply have desires I go to the **word** of God to find my direction and answers to my questions. I simply read, pray and believe. I read the bible and choose to trust. This is what I know has been verified to work. Just like David, I rely on my weapons that are proven to work. Let the following scriptures give you direction and strength!

-   "For I know the thoughts that I think toward you, saith the LORD, thoughts of peace, and not of evil, to give you an expected end." (Jeremiah 29:11)

- "For God hath not given us the spirit of fear; but of power and love, and of a sound mind." (II Timothy 1:7)

- "If ye abide in me, and my **word**s abide in you ye shall ask what ye will, and it shall be done unto you." (John 15:7)

- "Ye are of God, little children, and have overcome them: because greater is he that is in you, than he that is in the world." (I John 4:4)

- "For we are his workmanship, created in Christ Jesus unto good works, which God hath before ordained that we should walk in them." (Ephesians 2:10)

- Romans 6: 28-30

- 28. For we know that all things work together for good to them that love God, to them who are the called according to his purpose.

  29. For whom he did foreknow, he also did predestinate to be conformed to the image of his Son, that he might be the firstborn among many brethren.

  30. Moreover whom he did predestinate, them he also called and whom he called them he also justified: and whom he justified, them he also glorified.

- "The thief cometh not, but for to steal, and to kill, and to destroy: I am come that they might have life, and that they might have it more abundantly." (John 10:10)

67

- Proverbs 3: 5-6

5. Trust in the Lord with all thine heart; and lean not unto thine own understanding.

6. In all thy ways acknowledge him and he shall direct thy paths.

- Romans 6: 14-17

14. For as many as are led by the Spirit of God, they are the sons of God.

15. For ye have not received the spirit of bondage again to fear; but ye have received the Spirit of adoption, whereby we cry, Abba, Father.

16. The Spirit itself beareth witness with our spirit, that we are the children of God:

17. And if children, then heirs; heirs of God, and joint-heirs with Christ; if so be that we suffer with him, that we may be also glorified together.

- Psalms 139: 13-14

13. For thou hast possessed my reins thou has covered me in my mother's womb.

14. I will praise thee; for I am fearfully and wonderfully made: marvelous are thy works; and that my soul knoweth right well.

15. My substance was not hid from thee, when I was made in secret, and curiously wrought in secret in the lowest parts of the earth.

16. Thine eyes did see my substance, yet being imperfect; and in thy book all my members were written, which in continuance were fashioned, when as yet there was none of them.

17. How precious also are thy thoughts unto me, O God! How great is the sum of them!

18. If I should count them, they are more in number than sand: when I awake, I am still with thee.

- Ephesians 2:10

10. For we are his workmanship, created in Christ Jesus unto good works, which God hath before ordained that we should walk in them.

- "Who has saved us, and called us with an holy calling, not according to our works, but according to his own purpose and grace, which was given us in Christ Jesus before the world began," (II Timothy 1:9)

- "For the **word** of God is quick, and powerful, and sharper than any twoedged sword, piercing even to the dividing asunder of soul and spirit, and of the joints and marrow, and is a discerner of the thoughts and intents of the heart." (Hebrews 4:12)

God had delivered me and I walk in that deliverance today Thank you God. If it had not been for the grace of God where would I be?

CONCLUSION

A little over 10 years ago when I began to write this book at the time I wrote…. **I spent almost 26 years of my life trying to prove to those around me that I was good enough. I may have satisfied others but I myself was not satisfied. I had to realize that all I needed in order to be complete was to be accepted by my creator and accepted into God's family.** I am ready to reposition my life. I cannot allow the enemy to steal the second half of my life. Am I willing to fight through my addictions and curses, so that I do not settle for less? I must wake up from this apathetic sleep, lack of emotion, disinterest, and indifference.

<u>Here I am now…..delivered, at peace, walking in authority!</u>

Finally, I have awakened. I feel, I mourn, I love, and I am compassionate. I have told God YES so that I can be the best me and bless others on earth. God has raised me through his grace and mercy to be a whole woman. I am an awesome mom! I am successful in business. I am a giver. I am a good friend. I am a good relative. I am whatever God says that I am.

I am still humbly learning. I believe with my whole heart that when you are on this earth and you feel that you have arrived, know it all, and there is nothing more for you to learn then it is time for you to go home and meet your maker. If there is nothing left for you to do, no one left for you to bless, no one left for you to encourage, help, assist, teach, pray for, lend a hand to, then why are you here? That is the question that we must all ask ourselves again and again. Why are we here?

Wake up!!!! Take control of your life and destiny through God's **word** and his spirit. Fulfill the purpose that God has for you! What Legacy will you leave behind? Let your legacy eclipse all of your struggles and end with Eyes have not seen, Ears has not heard the things that God has been able to accomplish through your life here on earth! This is what I challenge you to do my brother, my sister.

What are you going to do to take back your life?

EYES HAVE NOT SEEN!..... EARS HAVE NOT HEARD!.....

WHAT WILL YOUR OBITUARY SAY?

Michelle Whitmore

.

EYES HAVE NOT SEEN!.....   EARS HAVE NOT HEARD!.....

www.ingramcontent.com/pod-product-compliance
Lightning Source LLC
Chambersburg PA
CBHW062023040426
42447CB00010B/2114